Super Green Smoothie Cookbook

Healthy Smoothie Recipes for a Healthier You

BY: Nancy Silverman

COPYRIGHT NOTICES

© 2019 Nancy Silverman All Rights Reserved

Subject to the agreement and permission of the author, this Book, in part or in whole, may not be reproduced in any format. This includes but is not limited to electronically, in print, scanning or photocopying.

The opinions, guidelines and suggestions written here are solely those of the Author and are for information purposes only. Every possible measure has been taken by the Author to ensure accuracy but let the Reader be advised that they assume all risk when following information. The Author does not assume any risk in the case of damages, personally or commercially, in the case of misinterpretation or misunderstanding while following any part of the Book.

My Heartfelt Thanks and A Special Reward for Your Purchase!

https://nancy.gr8.com

My heartfelt thanks at purchasing my book and I hope you enjoy it! As a special bonus, you will now be eligible to receive books absolutely free on a weekly basis! Get started by entering your email address in the box above to subscribe. A notification will be emailed to you of my free promotions, no purchase necessary! With little effort, you will be eligible for free and discounted books daily. In addition to this amazing gift, a reminder will be sent 1-2 days before the offer expires to remind you not to miss out. Enter now to start enjoying this special offer!

Table of Contents

(1) Zucchini and Raspberry Green Smoothie 7

(2) Apricot Cucumber Green Smoothie 9

(3) Watermelon Lettuce Smoothie 11

(4) Avocado Clementine Smoothie 13

(5) Very Berry Green Smoothie 15

(6) Banana Mint Green Smoothie 17

(7) Veggie-Only Green Smoothie 19

(8) Blueberry Mint Green Smoothie 21

(9) Vanilla, Apple, and Basil Smoothie 23

(10) Blueberry, Banana, Wheat Grass Smoothie 25

(11) Turmeric Super Cleanser Green Smoothie 27

(12) Calcium Packed Orange Smoothie 29

(13) Tropical Wheatgrass Green Smoothie 31

(14) Cherry Chocolate Green Smoothie 33

(15) Tropical Spicy Jalapeno Green Smoothie 35

(16) Cinnamon Spiced Pear and Blueberry 37

(17) Strawberry Papaya Green Smoothie 39

(18) Citrus, Cucumber, and Honeydew Smoothie 41

(19) Strawberry Lemonade Green Smoothie 43

(20) Coco, Peach, and Ginger Green Smoothie 45

(21) Stomach Soothing Green Smoothie 47

(22) Coconut and Clementine Green Smoothie 49

(23) Savory Sage Banana Smoothie Recipe 51

(24) Collard Greens with Lime and Mango 53

(25) Red Grape and Chia Seed Smoothie 55

(26) Grapefruit Green Smoothie 57

(27) Pumpkin Spiced Nutty Green Smoothie 59

(28) Green Goddess Protein Smoothie 61

(29) Pomegranate Cacao Green Smoothie 64

(30) Green Smoothie with Figs 66

(31) Pistachio Cream Pie 68

(32) Greener Colada Smoothie... 70

(33) Pineapple and Frozen Banana with Kale 72

(34) Guacamole Green Smoothie 74

(35) Peanut Protein Strawberry Smoothie 76

(36) Kickin' Kiwi Smoothie 78

(37) PB&B Green Smoothie 81

(38) Mango Green Smoothie.. 83

(39) Matcha Vanilla Protein Smoothie............................... 85

(40) Matcha Pear Protein Green Smoothie 87

About the Author... 89

Author's Afterthoughts.. 91

(1) Zucchini and Raspberry Green Smoothie

Zucchini is a great source of vitamin C. Incorporating it into your diet will help to prevent diseases caused by vitamin C deficiency, such as poor eyesight, easy bruising and even sclerosis.

Serving Sizes: 1

Preparation Time: 5 mins

Ingredient List:

- ½ zucchini
- ½ small cucumber
- 10-12 raspberries
- 1 cup baby spinach
- 8 ounces almond milk
- ½ frozen banana

Instructions:

- Add all ingredients into a blender and blitz for at least one minute until totally smooth. Pour into a glass and serve.

(2) Apricot Cucumber Green Smoothie

First cultivated in China thousands of years ago, people have been enjoying the health benefits of apricots for millenniums. Make this smoothie a part of your daily routine and enjoy healthier, brighter skin.

Serving Sizes: 1

Preparation Time: 5 mins

Ingredient List:

- 4 apricots (pitted)
- 1 small kiwi (peeled, chopped)
- ¼ medium cucumber (chopped)
- 1½ cups spinach
- 8 ounces almond milk

Instructions:

- Add all ingredients into a blender and blitz until totally smooth. Pour into a glass and serve.

(3) Watermelon Lettuce Smoothie

Simple ingredients in this easy to make recipe, with the added bonus that romaine lettuce is heart healthy.

Serving Sizes: 2

Preparation Time: 4 mins

Ingredient List:

- 3 cups watermelon chunks
- 5 romaine lettuce leaves
- 1 medium banana
- 1 small piece ginger
- Lemon juice (to taste)

Instructions:

- In a blender, combine all 5 ingredients and blitz until smooth.

(4) Avocado Clementine Smoothie

Avocado makes for a super thick and creamy smoothie without adding any overpowering flavor.

Serving Sizes: 2

Preparation Time: 5 mins

Ingredient List:

- 2 clementines
- 1 ripe fresh avocado (pitted, flesh scooped away from peel)
- 1 overripe banana (chopped)
- 1 cup almond milk
- 2 cups fresh spinach
- 1 Tablespoon raw honey

Instructions:

- Add all ingredients into a blender and blitz until smooth and very creamy. Pour into glasses and top with ice. Serve!

(5) Very Berry Green Smoothie

Detox, nourish, and enjoy your body with this delicious tasting drink.

Serving Sizes: 1

Preparation Time: 5 mins

Ingredient List:

- ½ cup unsweetened almond milk
- 4 ounces fresh spinach
- ½ cup fresh blueberries
- ½ cup fresh raspberries
- Stevia powder (optional)

Instructions:

- Add the first 4 ingredients to a food blender and blitz until smooth. Taste and add a little Stevia for sweetening if necessary.

(6) Banana Mint Green Smoothie

Creamy banana fuses with fresh mint to bring a totally refreshing take on a green smoothie.

Serving Sizes: 2

Preparation Time: 5 mins

Ingredient List:

- 1 large frozen banana
- 1 cup baby spinach
- ½ cup vanilla flavored low-fat Greek yogurt
- ½ cup skim milk
- ⅓ cup fresh mint leaves
- 4 ice cubes

Instructions:

- In a food blender, add the banana, spinach, vanilla yogurt, milk, mint leaves, and ice cubes. Blitz until silky.

(7) Veggie-Only Green Smoothie

For the hardened green smoothie drinker, we have this veggie-only version.

Serving Sizes: 1

Preparation Time: 5 mins

Ingredient List:

- 1 small zucchini (chopped)
- 1 tomato (chopped)
- 1 celery stalk (chopped)
- 1 sliver red onion (chopped)
- ½ garlic clove
- ½ tsp dried dill
- ⅛ tsp salt
- ⅛ tsp cayenne pepper
- 1¾ cups cold water*

Instructions:

- Add all ingredients into a blender and blitz for at least one minute until totally smooth. Pour into a glass and serve.
- You can use hot water instead of cold if you would prefer a warm, more soup-like smoothie.

(8) Blueberry Mint Green Smoothie

Mint and berries combined with spinach– a refreshing, energizing drink.

Serving Sizes: 1

Preparation Time: 3 mins

Ingredient List:

- 2 cups frozen spinach
- 2 cups fresh blueberries
- 1 kiwi
- 4 large mint leaves
- 1 cup coconut water
- 1 cup ice

Instructions:

- Add all 6 ingredients into a food blender and blitz until silky smooth.

(9) Vanilla, Apple, and Basil Smoothie

Vanilla almond milk and maple syrup make this basil apple smoothie super creamy and naturally sweet.

Serving Sizes: 1-2

Preparation Time: 3 mins

Ingredient List:

- 1 Fuji apple (chopped)
- ¾ cup vanilla almond milk
- 6 large basil leaves
- 1 Tablespoon pure maple syrup
- ½ teaspoon freshly squeezed lemon juice
- Ice

Instructions:

- Add all ingredients into a blender along with some ice and blitz until smooth. Pour into a glass and enjoy!

(10) Blueberry, Banana, Wheat Grass Smoothie

Wheat grass powder is the new best thing! It helps to detoxify the body and boosts the immune system. With apples providing fiber, bananas bringing potassium, and berries for antioxidants, this is a powerful smoothie.

Serving Sizes: 2

Preparation Time: 7 mins

Ingredient List:

- 1 Tablespoon wheatgrass powder
- 1 Tablespoon chia seeds
- 1 Tablespoon hemp seeds
- 1 Tablespoon flax powder
- 1 cup mixed green
- ½ cup carrot juice
- 1 cup almond milk
- 1 medium apple
- 1 medium banana
- ½ cup fresh blueberries

Instructions:

- Add all the ingredients to a food blender, in recipe ingredient order and blitz until silky.

(11) Turmeric Super Cleanser Green Smoothie

Lots of healthy ingredients are in this green smoothie. A natural detox in a glass.

Serving Sizes: 1

Preparation Time: 5 mins

Ingredient List:

- 2 cups fresh kale
- 2 cups fresh pineapple
- 2 cups coconut milk
- Juice of ½ lemon
- 1 cup fresh mango
- 1 Tablespoon fresh grated ginger
- ½ tsp ground turmeric

Instructions:

- In a food blender, blitz the kale and coconut milk until silky.
- Add the remaining 5 ingredients and blitz until smooth.

(12) Calcium Packed Orange Smoothie

Oranges will give you much needed Vitamin C, the banana provides potassium, and the kale is calcium rich.

Serving Sizes: 1

Preparation Time: 4 mins

Ingredient List:

- 4 ounces hazelnut milk
- 2 oranges (peeled)
- 1 medium banana (peeled)
- 2 cups kale (roughly chopped)

Instructions:

- First add the liquid to a food blender, followed by the fruit and then the kale. Blitz until smooth. Serve over ice cubes.

(13) Tropical Wheatgrass Green Smoothie

Wheatgrass has lots of vitamins and minerals, but doesn't taste so good. By including pineapple, bananas, and coconut milk in the smoothie, it will mellow out the distinctive flavor.

Serving Sizes: 1

Preparation Time: 4mins

Ingredient List:

- 2 cups fresh pineapple chunks
- 2 bananas
- 1 pack wheatgrass
- 1 cup baby spinach
- 8 ounces coconut water

Instructions:

- Add the liquid ingredients to a food blender and blitz. Next, add the fruit and finally the greens. Blitz on high speed for 30 seconds, or until the mixture is silky.

(14) Cherry Chocolate Green Smoothie

Adding raw cacao to smoothies is a great healthy way to get your chocolate fix and also nourish your body with antioxidants.

Serving Sizes: 1-2*

Preparation Time: 5 mins

Ingredient List:

- 8 ounces almond milk
- 1 ripe banana (chopped)
- 1 cup frozen pitted cherries
- 1 scoop flavored protein powder (chocolate or vanilla)
- 1 Tablespoon cacao powder
- 3 cups baby spinach

Instructions:

- Add all ingredients into a blender and blitz until smooth. Pour into a glass and serve.
- *This recipe makes one large serving or 2 small servings. This smoothie can be drunk as a meal replacement. We recommend drinking half and then reserving the rest to drink after 1 hour.

(15) Tropical Spicy Jalapeno Green Smoothie

Jalapeno is a great metabolism booster making this an ideal smoothie for anyone trying to lose a few pounds.

Serving Sizes: 2-3

Preparation Time: 5 mins

Ingredient List:

- 1 handful fresh baby spinach
- 1 fresh mango (cut into chunks)
- 1 cup coconut water
- 1 cup cucumber (roughly chopped)
- ¼ jalapeno (deseeded, chopped)
- 1 handful fresh cilantro
- 2 sprigs fresh mint
- Juice of 1 lime
- Ice

Instructions:

- Add all ingredients into a blender along with a few ice cubes and blitz until smooth. Pour into glasses and serve!

(16) Cinnamon Spiced Pear and Blueberry

The ingredients in this smoothie contain a powerful dose of calcium, potassium, and magnesium, which are a winning combination for lowering blood pressure.

Serving Sizes: 1-2

Preparation Time: 5 mins

Ingredient List:

- 1 medium pear (peeled, chopped)
- 1 cup fresh blueberries
- ½ tsp cinnamon
- 8 ounces almond milk
- 2 cups spinach
- Ice cubes

IIIIIIIIIIIIIIIIIIIIIIIIIIIIIIIIIIIIIIIIIIIIIII

Instructions:

- Add all ingredients, excluding the spinach, into a blender and blitz until smooth. Add in the spinach along with a few ice cubes and blend again until totally combined. Pour into a glass and serve.

(17) Strawberry Papaya Green Smoothie

Sweet strawberries and tropical papaya make a yummy green kale smoothie, that's also low carb!

Serving Sizes: 1

Preparation Time: 5 mins

Ingredient List:

- ½ cup fresh papaya (chopped)
- 8 fresh strawberries
- ½ ripe banana
- 8 ounces almond milk
- 2 cups kale

Instructions:

- Add all ingredients into a blender along with a few ice cubes and blitz until smooth. Pour into a glass and serve.

(18) Citrus, Cucumber, and Honeydew Smoothie

Cucumber and fresh mint make for a garden-fresh smoothie, while honeydew melon and fresh orange juice naturally sweeten.

Serving Sizes: 1

Preparation Time: 3 mins

Ingredient List:

- 2 cups fresh spinach
- 1 cup honeydew melon (chopped)
- 2" segment fresh cucumber (peeled)
- Freshly squeezed juice from ½ large orange
- Small handful fresh mint
- Ice cubes

Instructions:

- Add all ingredients into a blender and blitz until smooth. Pour into a glass and serve topped up with a few ice cubes!

(19) Strawberry Lemonade Green Smoothie

Tangy and sweet, just how a good lemonade should be. Our version also comes packed with chia seeds and collard greens for double the health benefits.

Serving Sizes: 1

Preparation Time: 5 mins

Ingredient List:

- 5-6 strawberries
- ¼ medium lemon (peeled, deseeded)
- 1 banana
- 2 stemless collard leaves
- 1 Tablespoon soaked chia seeds
- 8 ounces almond milk

Instructions:

- Add all ingredients into a blender and blitz until totally smooth. Pour into a glass and serve.

(20) Coco, Peach, and Ginger Green Smoothie

Ginger brings a mild heat as well as immune system boosting properties. A great smoothie if you have the sniffles or feel they are on their way.

Serving Sizes: 2

Preparation Time: 5 mins

Ingredient List:

- 1 cup fresh peach (sliced)
- 2-3 ice cubes
- ½ banana (sliced, frozen)
- ¾ cup coconut water
- ½ tsp ginger (grated)
- 1 tsp honey

Instructions:

- Add all ingredients into a blender along with a few ice cubes and blitz until smooth. Pour into glasses and serve!

(21) Stomach Soothing Green Smoothie

Are you suffering from tummy troubles? If you are, the turmeric and ginger in this smoothie will help to alleviate swelling.

Serving Sizes: 1

Preparation Time: 3 mins

Ingredient List:

- 2 cups spinach
- 2 cups cold water
- 3 cups fresh pineapple (chopped)
- Juice of 1 lemon
- ½ tsp ground turmeric
- ½" fresh ginger (peeled)

Instructions:

- In a food blender, combine the spinach with the cold water and blitz until smooth. Add the remaining ingredients and blitz again.

(22) Coconut and Clementine Green Smoothie

A creamy non-dairy breakfast beverage that will satisfy not only your hunger, but also your taste buds. Enjoy.

Serving Sizes: 2

Preparation Time: 5 mins

Ingredient List:

- 4-5 clementines (peeled, stringed)
- 1 ripe banana (sliced, frozen)
- ½ cup light coconut milk
- 1 big handful spinach
- 4 ice cubes

Instructions:

- In a food blender, combine all ingredients and blitz until silky.

(23) Savory Sage Banana Smoothie Recipe

By adding sage to this recipe, you are enjoying its many health benefits. This herb is an excellent source of Vitamin A, fiber, iron, calcium, and magnesium, to name but a few.

Serving Sizes: 1

Preparation Time: 4 mins

Ingredient List:

- 1 cup almond milk
- I cup spinach
- 1 ripe banana
- 3 sage leaves (chopped)
- ¼ tsp ground cinnamon
- ½ tsp pure maple syrup
- 4 ice cubes (optional)

Instructions:

- Put all 7 ingredients into a food blender and blitz until silky.

(24) Collard Greens with Lime and Mango

Tangy and flavorsome. If you are looking for a protein-packed shake, add a little whey protein.

Serving Sizes: 2

Preparation Time: 5 mins

Ingredient List:

- 2 tablespoons freshly squeezed lime juice
- 2 cups collard greens (chopped)
- 1½ cups frozen mango
- 1 cup green grapes

Instructions:

- In a food blender, combine all 4 ingredients and blitz until silky. Add a little water if you find the consistency too thick.

(25) Red Grape and Chia Seed Smoothie

Chia seeds are a great ingredient to add to your smoothie if you're hoping to lose weight. They're packed with fiber and will help you to feel fuller for longer.

Serving Sizes: 1

Preparation Time: 5 mins

Ingredient List:

- ½ cup seedless red grapes
- 2 tsp. soaked chia seeds
- 1 ripe banana
- ¼ avocado (pitted)
- ½ small cucumber (chopped)
- ½ scoop vanilla protein powder
- 4 ounces almond milk
- 2 cups stemless kale

Instructions:

- Add all ingredients, excluding the kale, into a blender and blitz until smooth. Add in the kale along with a few ice cubes and blend again until totally combined. Pour into a glass and serve.

(26) Grapefruit Green Smoothie

They say you either love or hate grapefruit. If you're a fan, then this is the smoothie for you. Bittersweet and zesty, wake yourself up with this green blend.

Serving Sizes: 1

Preparation Time: 5mins

Ingredient List:

- ½ yellow grapefruit (deseeded, peeled)
- ½ frozen banana
- 1 cup spinach
- 4 ounces almond milk

Instructions:

- Add all ingredients into a blender and blitz until totally smooth. Pour into a glass and serve.

(27) Pumpkin Spiced Nutty Green Smoothie

The ultimate Fall smoothie. Comforting pumpkin spice and hazelnuts give a pumpkin pie flavor to this filling green smoothie.

Serving Sizes: 1*

Preparation Time: 5mins

Ingredient List:

- 8 ounces almond milk
- ½ cup pureed pumpkin
- 1 ripe banana
- 10 hazelnuts
- 1 scoop vanilla protein powder
- ½ tsp ground cinnamon
- ¼ tsp ground nutmeg
- 2 handfuls spinach

Instructions:

- Add all ingredients, excluding the spinach, into a blender and blitz until smooth. Add in the spinach along with a few ice cubes and blend again until totally combined. Pour into a glass and serve.
- This recipe makes one large smoothie which should be enjoyed as a breakfast or lunch replacement, rather than a snack.

(28) Green Goddess Protein Smoothie

Gluten free and vegan-friendly this smoothie is basically a meal in a glass.

Serving Sizes: 2

Preparation Time: 9mins

Ingredient List:

- ½ cup fresh red grapefruit juice
- 1 cup baby spinach
- 1 large sweet apple (cored, chopped)
- 1 cup cucumber (chopped)
- 1 medium/large stalk celery (chopped)
- 4 tablespoons hemp hearts
- ⅓ cup frozen mango
- 2 tablespoons packed fresh mint leaves
- 1½ tsp virgin coconut oil
- 4 ice cubes

Instructions:

- Add the grapefruit juice to a food blender. Next, add in the baby spinach, chopped apple, cucumber, celery, hemp hearts, frozen mango, mint leaves, coconut oil, and ice. Blitz on high until silky.
- Add a drop of cold water if you feel you need a less thick consistency.

(29) Pomegranate Cacao Green Smoothie

Pomegranate and cacao make an indulgent tasty smoothie while spinach provides important health promoting antioxidants.

Serving Sizes: 1-2*

Preparation Time: 5mins

Ingredient List:

- ½ cup pomegranate fruit
- 1 cup blueberries
- 1 frozen banana
- ½ cup raspberries
- 1 Tablespoon cacao powder
- 8 ounces almond milk
- 3 cups spinach

Instructions:

- Add all ingredients, excluding the spinach, into a blender and blitz until smooth. Add in the spinach and blend again until totally combined. Pour into a glass and serve.
- This recipe makes one large serving or 2 small servings. This smoothie can be drunk as a meal replacement. We recommend drinking half and then reserving the rest to drink after 1 hour.

(30) Green Smoothie with Figs

Figs are fiber-rich and so great for your digestion. But did you know that in every serving of avocado there are nearly 20 minerals and vitamins?

Serving Sizes: 1

Preparation Time: 4 mins

Ingredient List:

- 1 cup coconut water
- 2 fresh figs (pitted)
- ⅓ avocado
- 2 handfuls kale
- 2 dates
- Juice of ½ lime
- Handful of ice

Instructions:

- Add all 7 ingredients to a food blender and blitz until silky.

(31) Pistachio Cream Pie

A really creamy treat but still bursting with goodness.

Serving Sizes: 1

Preparation Time: 4 mins

Ingredient List:

- 1½ ounces kale
- 1 banana
- ½ avocado (pitted)
- 1 Tablespoon pistachios
- ½ tsp spirulina
- 1 cup vanilla almond milk
- 1 cup ice

Instructions:

- Blitz all the ingredients in a food blender and enjoy.

(32) Greener Colada Smoothie

A healthy non-alcoholic take on a Pina Colada. All the tropical flavors with added health benefits. Scrumptious!

Serving Sizes: 1

Preparation Time: 5 mins

Ingredient List:

- 1 cup fat-free Greek yogurt
- 1 cup frozen pineapple
- 1 cup kale
- ½ cup low-fat coconut milk
- ½ tsp vanilla extract
- Unsweetened coconut flakes (for garnish)

||||||||||||||||||||||||||||||||||||||||||||

Instructions:

- In a food blender, combine the Greek yogurt, frozen pineapple, kale, coconut milk, and vanilla.
- Blitz until silky and garnish with coconut flakes before serving.

(33) Pineapple and Frozen Banana with Kale

No fancy powders or nut butter, just 4 simple readily available ingredients.

Serving Sizes: 2

Preparation Time: 5 mins

Ingredient List:

- ¾ cup almond or soy milk
- 2 bananas (sliced and frozen)
- 2 cups pineapple (cut into chunks)
- 2 cups fresh kale

Instructions:

- milk if the smoothie is a little thick. Pour into glasses and top with ice. Enjoy!

(34) Guacamole Green Smoothie

The epitome of Green Smoothies– kale, avocado, and a small kick of cayenne.

Serving Sizes: 1

Preparation Time: 4 mins

Ingredient List:

- ½ cup cold water
- 1 avocado (pitted)
- ½ cup tomatoes
- ¼ cup cilantro
- Juice of ½ lime
- Dash of sea salt
- 1 cup kale
- ¼ tsp cayenne pepper

Instructions:

- Add all ingredients to a food blender and blitz until silky.

(35) Peanut Protein Strawberry Smoothie

Lots of protein in this recipe— thanks to the peanut butter. This smoothie is so delicious it can be enjoyed as a dessert.

Serving Sizes: 1

Preparation Time: 3 mins

Ingredient List:

- ⅓ cup fat-free plain Greek yogurt
- ½ cup low-fat milk
- 1 cup baby spinach
- ½ cup frozen strawberries
- 1 cup frozen banana (sliced)
- 1 Tablespoon organic smooth peanut butter
- 1-2 tsp pure maple syrup

Instructions:

- First add the low-fat milk and Greek yogurt to a food blender, then add baby spinach, frozen banana, strawberries, peanut butter, and maple syrup. Blitz until creamy.

(36) Kickin' Kiwi Smoothie

Kick start your morning with this herby kiwi smoothie bursting with vitamins and minerals, as well as iron, calcium, and protein!

Serving Sizes: 2*

Preparation Time: 5 mins

Ingredient List:

- 1 frozen banana
- 1 small kiwi (peeled, chopped)
- 3 tablespoons goji berries
- 1 Tablespoon cacao powder
- 1 celery stalk (chopped)
- 8 ounces coconut water
- 1 scoop vanilla protein powder
- ½ cup parsley
- 1 cup spinach

Instructions:

- Add all ingredients, excluding the parsley and spinach, into a blender and blitz until smooth. Add the parsley and spinach, along with a few ice cubes and blend again until totally combined. Pour into a glass and serve.
- This smoothie can be drunk as a meal replacement. We recommend drinking half and then reserving the rest to drink after 1 hour.

(37) PB&B Green Smoothie

Peanut butter and banana do a great job of masking the taste of spinach. Great if you are not a fan of strong-tasting green smoothies but still want to reap the health benefits.

Serving Sizes: 2

Preparation Time: 3 mins

Ingredient List:

- 1 cup fresh spinach
- ½ ripe banana (chopped)
- ½ cup skim milk
- ¼ cup full-fat Greek yogurt
- ¼ tsp vanilla essence
- 1 tsp smooth peanut butter
- 1 tsp honey

Instructions:

- Add all ingredients into a blender along with a few ice cubes and blitz until smooth. Pour into glasses and serve!

(38) Mango Green Smoothie

A healthy green smoothie featuring mango and rolled oats. A great kick start to the day.

Serving Sizes: 4

Preparation Time: 5 mins

Ingredient List:

- 1½ cups cold water
- 2 medium oranges (peeled)
- 4 cups fresh spinach
- 4 cups frozen* or fresh mango
- ½ cup rolled oats

Instructions:

- In a food blender, blitz the oranges and water until silky.
- Add the remaining 3 ingredients and blitz until smooth.
- Using frozen mango will make the smoothie a lot colder.

(39) Matcha Vanilla Protein Smoothie

Matcha powder has more antioxidants than green tea. So you get a huge dose of health benefits in one simple glass.

Serving Sizes: 1

Preparation Time: 3 mins

Ingredient List:

- 1 cup almond milk
- 2 scoops vanilla protein powder of choice
- ½ cup ice
- 1 banana
- 2 tsp matcha green tea powder
- ½ tsp pure maple syrup
- Scrapings of 1 vanilla pod

Instructions:

- In a food blender blitz all ingredients until silky and serve.

(40) Matcha Pear Protein Green Smoothie

Matcha is one of the latest superfoods to hit the street. Lots of protein in this drink.

Serving Sizes: 1

Preparation Time: 5 mins

Ingredient List:

- 1 packet vanilla protein powder of choice
- 1 cup unsweetened almond milk
- 1 pear (cored)
- 1 cup spinach
- ½ tsp matcha tea powder

Instructions:

- In a food, blender combine all 5 ingredients and blitz until silky.

About the Author

Nancy Silverman is an accomplished chef from Essex, Vermont. Armed with her degree in Nutrition and Food Sciences from the University of Vermont, Nancy has excelled at creating e-books that contain healthy and delicious meals that anyone can make and everyone can enjoy. She improved her cooking skills at the New England Culinary Institute in Montpelier Vermont and she has been working at perfecting her culinary style since graduation. She claims that her life's work is always a work in progress and she only hopes to be an inspiration to aspiring chefs everywhere.

Her greatest joy is cooking in her modern kitchen with her family and creating inspiring and delicious meals. She often says that she has perfected her signature dishes based on her family's critique of each and every one.

Nancy has her own catering company and has also been fortunate enough to be head chef at some of Vermont's most exclusive restaurants. When a friend suggested she share some of her outstanding signature dishes, she decided to add cookbook author to her repertoire of personal achievements. Being a technological savvy woman, she felt the e-book realm would be a better fit and soon she had her first cookbook available online. As of today, Nancy has sold over 1,000 e-books and has shared her culinary experiences and brilliant recipes with people from all over the world! She plans on expanding into self-help books and dietary cookbooks, so stayed tuned!

Author's Afterthoughts

Thank you for making the decision to invest in one of my cookbooks! I cherish all my readers and hope you find joy in preparing these meals as I have.

There are so many books available and I am truly grateful that you decided to buy this one and follow it from beginning to end.

I love hearing from my readers on what they thought of this book and any value they received from reading it. As a personal favor, I would appreciate any feedback you can give in the form of a review on Amazon and please be honest! This kind of support will help others make an informed choice on and will help me tremendously in producing the best quality books possible.

My most heartfelt thanks,

Nancy Silverman

If you're interested in more of my books, be sure to follow my author page on Amazon (can be found on the link Bellow) or scan the QR-Code.

https://www.amazon.com/author/nancy-silverman

Made in the USA
Las Vegas, NV
27 June 2025